COMPENDIUM OF CHORDS FOR THE VIOLA

BENJAMIN WHITCOMB

authorHOUSE®

AuthorHouse™
1663 Liberty Drive
Bloomington, IN 47403
www.authorhouse.com
Phone: 1 (800) 839-8640

Published by AuthorHouse 03/26/2018

ISBN: 978-1-5462-3071-7 (sc)
ISBN: 978-1-5462-3070-0 (e)

Print information available on the last page.

This book is printed on acid-free paper.

Because of the dynamic nature of the Internet, any web addresses or links contained in this book may have changed since publication and may no longer be valid. The views expressed in this work are solely those of the author and do not necessarily reflect the views of the publisher, and the publisher hereby disclaims any responsibility for them.

Contents

Acknowledgments

There are many people who helped me write this book, whether they realize it or not. First of all, I would never have been able to have written a book such as this without my primary cello teachers, Monty Lawson, Evan Tonsing, George Neikrug, and Phyllis Young.

I am extremely grateful for the useful suggestions and advice from the people who helped review this work, including Anne Witt, Tess Remy-Schumacher, Linda Jennings, Leanne League, Rebecca MacLeod, and Laurie Scott. I would also like to thank my parents, Carl and LaJean Whitcomb, my sons, Spencer and Preston, and my wife Pamela, for everything.

Introduction

There are many resources for practicing scales and arpeggios on the viola, but extremely few for practicing chords. Understanding chords on the viola can be a very useful skill for a variety of reasons, the most obvious of which is that chords appear a significant number of times in the viola repertoire. In addition, understanding chords:

- helps you to think harmonically
- helps you to better analyze music
- improves your ability to sight read and to play arpeggios and double stops
- helps the fingers of your left hand to work better together as a team
- facilitates composition and improvisation

Let us look at each of these reasons in turn.

Understanding chords helps you to think harmonically.

> The harmonic component of music follows various "rules" (i.e., tendencies and patterns) that are different from what melodies tend to do. The more time you spend familiarizing yourself with these tendencies, the more likely you are to set up habits of thought that allow you to anticipate and understand what is happening in such passages.

Understanding chords helps you to better analyze music.

> As important and salient as melody is in music, in most pieces the harmonic component plays an even bigger role in defining the musical form, structure, and function. Indeed, it is very difficult to understand an analysis of a piece of music without understanding chords.

Understanding chords improves your ability to sight read and to play arpeggios and double stops.

> Good sight reading involves the ability to see patterns, and to grab *groups* of notes with the brain (as opposed to one note at a time). Studying chords teaches us to think in terms of these patterns in groups. In addition, arpeggios and double stops are essentially derived from chords.

Understanding chords helps the fingers of your left hand to work better together as a team.

> By thinking of the groupings of notes that comprise chords, and accordingly forming hand shapes to play them, the left hand fingers get trained to work together as a team. The alternative, in which the left hand plays with an "every finger for itself" approach, is detrimental to the development of good left-hand technique.

Understanding chords facilitates composition and improvisation.

There are two types of musicians: those who like to compose or improvise, and those who do not. In my experience, one of the main differences between the two groups is that the former tend to have *harmonically intuitive* ears. This thing I call harmonic intuition is something that can be learned, and the best way to teach yourself this skill is to listen to all manner of chords and chord progressions while the brain is contemplating them.

In addition, understanding chords may allow you to accompany others (or even your own singing) in a manner typically reserved for the other "chordal" instruments.

For all these benefits, it is perhaps surprising that there are not more resources for learning chords on the viola, but the purpose of this text is to fill this niche.

We will start our journey by looking at various ways to play chords on the viola, such as by rolling them in different patterns. In part 1, the various types of chords are introduced, along with their inversions and the forms in which they often tend to appear on viola. Part 2 shows the most useful chord progressions in each of the major and minor keys. Part 3 explains some additional concepts and applications related to chords, along with some more advanced materials.

Preliminaries

Double-, triple-, or quadruple-stop chords?

On the viola, we typically encounter chords as triple or quadruple stops, but sometimes as double stops.

Double stops have the disadvantage of leaving out a chord member. Furthermore, a number of resources exist for practicing double-stop sixths and thirds on the viola. After you have studied the concept of chords on the viola in this volume, you will understand how to apply your knowledge of chord progressions to double stop sixths and thirds.

Quadruple stops are less common on the viola than triple stops, and they have the disadvantage of being more awkward in many cases. For example, quadruple stops in B major already start quite high on the fingerboard. Furthermore, the addition of the fourth pitch often offers little benefit, since even four-note chords can be played as triple stops (usually by omitting the fifth of the chord).

As such, for the purposes of this book, we will focus on chords as triple stops.

Triads and their inversions

A basic understanding of the concepts of triads and inversions is necessary for understanding this book. I will briefly explain them here, but if this explanation is insufficient, you should get yourself an introductory-level book on music theory.

A triad is a collection of three notes. In Western music, most triads are "tertian," meaning that they consist of pitches that are a third apart, such as in the following example.

When the pitches are stacked like this (three adjacent lines or three adjacent spaces), the bottom note is called the "root," the middle note is called the "third," and the top note is called the "fifth." Any time that the root is in the bass (i.e., is the lowest sounding note), the chord is said to be in "root position." If the third is in the bass, the chord is said to be in "first inversion." If the fifth is in the bass, the chord is in "second inversion." These inversion names hold true regardless of the arrangement of the other pitches in the chord. So, for example, all of the following are considered to be first inversion chords:

As you can see, some of the triads above would be easier to play on the viola than others. As you might expect, we will indeed favor showing the versions of the triads (sometimes called "voicings") which are easiest to play on and most commonly used with the viola.

In addition to triads, we can also have "seventh chords," which involves taking a triad and stacking one additional third on top, such as the following:

Ways to play chords on the viola

When we actually see a chord notated as a triple or quadruple stop on the viola, surely our first instinct is to play it as a quick roll, with the bottom two notes being played as a grace note to the upper two.

However, in the viola repertoire we find many other ways to perform chords. For example, sometimes the chord is rolled in one of the following manners:

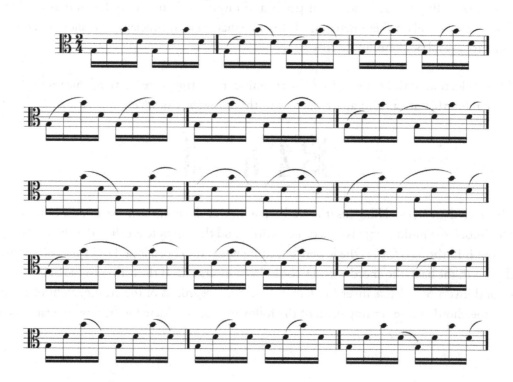

We also might encounter the chord with one or more of its pitches repeated:

Other times, the order of the notes in the chord is rearranged or permuted in various ways:

Familiarize yourself with all of the patterns above, since you are sure to encounter them in the repertoire. In addition, you will probably find it beneficial to vary the way that you play the chords presented in this book, as a way to keep the mind better engaged and the right hand challenged.

Part 1

Types of Chords

There are four types of tertian (i.e., consisting of notes a third apart) triads: major, minor, diminished, and augmented. We will address them in this order.

Major triads

In Western music, there are twelve half-steps within every octave. If we assume enharmonic equivalence (i.e., that F# = Gb, etc.), then there are twelve major chords that we can play:

```
1    2    2    2
0    1    1    1
0    1    1    1
```

If we were to go any further, we would start repeating the same chords an octave higher.

Whenever you find yourself playing a group of notes within a position with the fingering 1-1-2 (reading from bottom to top), with a whole step between 1 and 2, you know that you are playing a major triad. Of course, the same notes can be played with other fingerings like 2-2-3, but 1-1-2 is likely the fingering that you will most often associate with root position major chords.

Below is an example of a tablature-style representation of a major chord in first position. The left-most line represents the C string and the right-most, the A. The top line represents the nut, and each lower line thereafter represents another half-step distance from the nut. The black dots represent where to place the fingers.

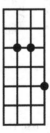

I hope that the illustrations like this in this chapter may further the brain's understanding of the chord *as a single shape of the hand.*

Inverted chords

In all of the chords above, the root is in the bass (i.e., the lowest sounding voice). Naturally, it is also possible to have the third of the chord in the bass ("first inversion" chords) or the fifth in the bass ("second inversion chords"). Below are the same chords as above, but in first inversion:

First inversion triads are used quite frequently in music, especially classical music. From now on, you will associate the fingering 1-2-2 (or 2-3-3 or 3-4-4), with a half step between the adjacent fingers, with first inversion major triads. Below is an illustration of this type of chord on a fingerboard:

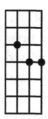

Here is the same collection of chords in second inversion:

For second inversion triads, you will most likely use the fingering 1-2-3 (or 2-3-4), with a whole step on bottom and a half step on top. Below is an illustration of the finger placement for these chords:

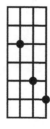

2

Minor triads

Here are the twelve minor triads in root position:

As you can see, the typical fingering here is 1-1-2, with a half step between 1 and 2. 2-2-3 and 3-3-4 work as well. Below is an illustration of a root position minor triad on the fingerboard:

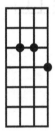

Here are the same minor triads but in first inversion:

Your most common fingering here would be 1-2-2, with a whole step between 1 and 2, although 2-3-3 and 3-4-4 can also work. Below is an illustration on the fingerboard:

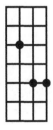

Here are the second inversion minor triads:

Note that the most common fingering for these is 1-2-3 (or 2-3-4), with a half step on bottom and a whole step on top. One such chord is shown on the fingerboard below:

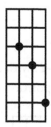

Diminished chords

There are two fingerings that we commonly encounter for diminished chords, as shown below:

The voicing above looks like this on a fingerboard:

Here is what this voicing looks like on a fingerboard:

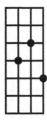

Notice the similarity of the pattern: 1-3-2 vs. 2-1-3. Be sure to practice both patterns so that your fingers do not get them confused.

The next most common voicing is the following:

Here, the fingering is 1-2-3, with whole steps between adjacent fingers, which is also shown in the illustration below:

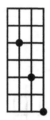

You will note that I am not discussing the diminished triad in terms of its inversions. This is because, when we encounter any of the diminished triads shown above in the viola repertoire, it often represents three of the four notes of a *diminished seventh chord*. For various reasons, diminished seventh chords are at least as common on the viola as diminished triads, and they are often used interchangeably. As such, it is generally simpler to think of each of the three fingerings above as equally representing diminished triads and diminished seventh chords.

Augmented triads

Augmented triads are the least common of them all, although you will occasionally find a work in which the composer has used them fairly liberally. Do not let their uncommon occurrence discourage you from practicing them.

Generally, we tend to find augmented triads voiced in the following manner:

The typical fingering for these chords would be 1-2-3 or 2-3-4, with half steps between adjacent fingers. One such chord is shown in the illustration below:

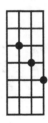

Dominant seventh chords

In addition to triads, there are various types of seventh chords that we could learn as well. However, some seventh chords are much more common than others, and we will restrict our discussion to the two most common: dominant seventh chords and diminished seventh chords. We addressed diminished seventh chords above, and presently we will address dominant seventh chords.

Dominant seventh chords consist of a major triad with the addition of a minor seventh (above the root of the chord). They are usually built on the fifth note of the scale, which is called the "dominant," thus the name "dominant seventh chord."

Dominant seventh chords tend to be encountered in one of three voicings, as shown below:

Of these three, the third is rarely encountered. The first fingering is quite common, and one such example is shown in the illustration below:

Introduction to chord progressions

We now know the various common types of triads and seventh chords, but what comes next? Real music consists of a series of different chords, which is called a chord progression. The best way to understand how one chord moves to the next is generally in terms of the interval between the roots of the chords.

If you are familiar with the concept of *interval inversions*, you know that you can get to the same pitch by going up a second (i.e., C up to D) as by going down a seventh (i.e., C *down* to D). Similarly, a third one direction (i.e., C up to E) is the same as a sixth the other (i.e., C down to E), and a fourth one way (i.e., C up to F) is the same as a fifth the other (i.e., C down to F). As such, we only need to study three different types of root movement: movement by second, by third, and by fifth.

Pattern of chord qualities

When we form root position diatonic triads on each scale degree of a major or minor scale, we see that the pattern of chord qualities is always the same. In a major key, the pattern is the following:

This pattern is worth committing to memory. On the viola, we often divide the scale into two tetrachords (groups of four notes) and cross strings between the two groups. In the case of the major scale, the pattern of qualities of the two tetrachords is almost the same:

      M m m M
      M m o M

which aids in memorization of the pattern.

In minor keys, there is no such symmetry between the two tetrachords, alas:

Note that this pattern is created by using harmonic minor for the V and viio chords (the "dominant function" chords). Other patterns of qualities can be formed by using natural of melodic minor, but the pattern above is the most common for harmonies in minor keys.

The "rule of the octave"

The patterns shown above are for all root-position triads, but in actual music we are free to use inverted triads as well. How should you decide when to use an inverted chord? You may, of course, let your ear be your guide. For many musicians throughout history, our ears have guided us to favor replacing chords with weaker harmonics function (such as iii chords) with strong ones (such as I or V). In the 18th century, J. P. Rameau devised a simple system of guidelines for harmonizing (i.e., setting chords to) each of the notes of a major or minor scale, which at that time was called the "règle de l'loctave" (rule of the octave). In my opinion, Rameau's approach to creating a default harmonization for stepwise progressions has not been substantially improved upon since, so it is the approach I will use here.

Below, such a progression is shown for C major and C minor:

As you can see, most of the notes of the scale are harmonized as the root of a triad, the exceptions being that the scale degrees that are members of the tonic triad (1, 3, and 5) or the dominant triad (5, 7, and 2) tend to be harmonized as either a tonic or dominant chord, even when the result is an inverted chord.

Variants of the progression above include replacing the viio chord with a V64, or replacing the IV chord with a ii6, such as in the following examples:

In general, these pairs of chords are interchangeable (viio6 with V64; IV with ii6), and they will be used in this way in this book. In the context of any particular musical passage, you will probably prefer one or the other, depending on factors like voice leading or the chord quality. In order to be as flexible of a player as possible, you should strive to eventually become equally comfortable with either option.

We can also create a chromatic "rule of the octave" progression, in which each of the twelve chromatic pitches is harmonized in a way that makes the most functional sense in terms of C major:

The idea here is that, if you wanted to have a functional-sounding chord progression combined with the melodic pull of a stepwise or chromatic bass line, the "rule of the octave" progressions above could provide you with a possible solution—something relatively easy to remember that you knew would work at least reasonably well.

The circle of fifths

In many styles of Western music, the most common type of chord progression is through the "circle of fifths." You could, of course, think of the same progression as being a "circle of fourths," but the name "circle of fifths" is what it became known as 300 years ago, and we have been referring to this type of progression by this name ever since.

Below is an example of a circle of fifths progression in C major and C minor:

i   iv   VII   III   VI   iio   V   i

Notice that this progression involves going down a fifth (or up a fourth). While it is possible to find examples of circle-of-fifths progressions that go the other direction (up a fifth/down a fourth), they are decidedly less common.

A more chromatic version of the circle of fifths can be created by turning all of the chords into major chords (or even into dominant seventh chords). For example:

I   IV   V/iii   V/vi   V/ii   V/V   V   I

The circle of thirds

While the "circle of thirds" is discussed in the music theory literature far less than the circle of fifths, it is an important concept nonetheless. Below is an example of a circle-of-thirds progression in C major and c minor:

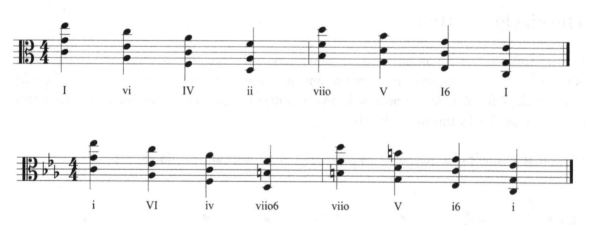

I   vi   IV   ii   viio   V   I6   I

i   VI   iv   viio6   viio   V   i6   i

Note that, as with the circle of fifths progression, the circle of thirds most commonly involves *descending* thirds.

Sometimes the circle-of-thirds progression involves embellishing each chord with the one a step below it, as in the following example:

I   V   vi   iii   IV   V6/ii   ii   vi   viio   V6/V   V   viio6   I6   viio   I

Chord progressions with suspensions

Sometimes chord progressions are embellished through other means, such as by adding non-chord tones (i.e., notes that are not part of the harmony). While several types of non-chord tones exist (such as passing tones, neighbor tones, escape tones, appoggiaturas, and pedal tones), arguably the most useful ones to understand are suspensions, which involve delaying the resolution of one (or sometimes two) chord tones until after the other notes have already moved to the new chord.

Below is an example of a chord progression with suspensions: the top note has been "suspended" by delaying its resolution until the lower two notes have changed chords.

I   viio   vi   V   IV   iii   ii   I

Here is an example in which the middle note has been suspended:

Below is an example in which the lowest note has the suspensions:

Part 2:

The basic chord progressions in all keys

The next step is to transpose these chord progressions into all major and minor keys. Most of you could surely do this "by rote," and indeed one of your goals should be to eventually learn to play these chords without the need for music. However, there is also something to be said for reading these chords—familiarizing your eyes with what they look like on the page. In addition, learning them first by reading them will probably speed up the learning process for most players.

You could progress through the keys in any number of orders but, to me, it makes the most sense to begin with C major and minor and then to ascend chromatically through the remaining keys. For your convenience, I have also included all enharmonic keys as well.

For each key, I begin with a series of short progressions that you are likely to encounter in many styles of music, followed by "rule of the octave," circle of thirds, and circle of fifths progressions. Do feel free to substitute other voicings, spacings, or registers of the chords as you see fit. You may also wish to add fingerings, particularly for the more remote keys.

If you do add fingerings, try to transition away from writing one for every note. Instead, try only writing a fingering when you feel you need to, such as when a pattern changes or to remind yourself of a particular finger spacing. In my system of marking fingerings, Roman numerals refer to the various strings and the letters L and H refer respectively to low or high position within the hand shape. Feel free to develop your own system of notating fingerings, but be sure that it is clear and consistent.

Opposite the page of block chords is a series of two-octave arpeggios corresponding to each of the three longer progressions ("rule of the octave," circle of thirds, and circle of fifths), since these provide another useful way to learn these patterns and progressions. You may wish to add fingerings to these as well. I would recommend keeping the pattern as similar as possible.

I recommend marking as few fingerings as possible. Writing in too many fingerings becomes somewhat of a mental crutch and can slow down your brain's ability to think of the notes in groups. Try erasing some or all of the fingerings as soon as you feel able to do so. In addition, you might try alternating between playing a progression with the music and then without.

C Major

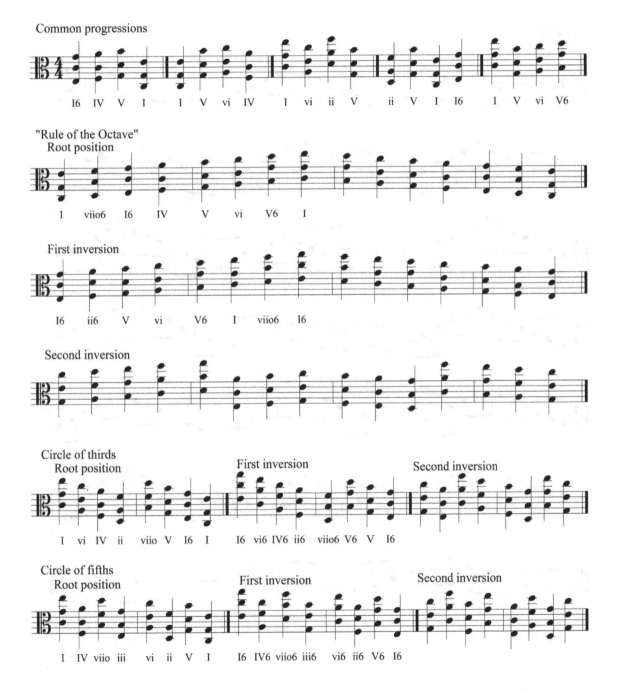

Arpeggios

"Rule of the Octave"

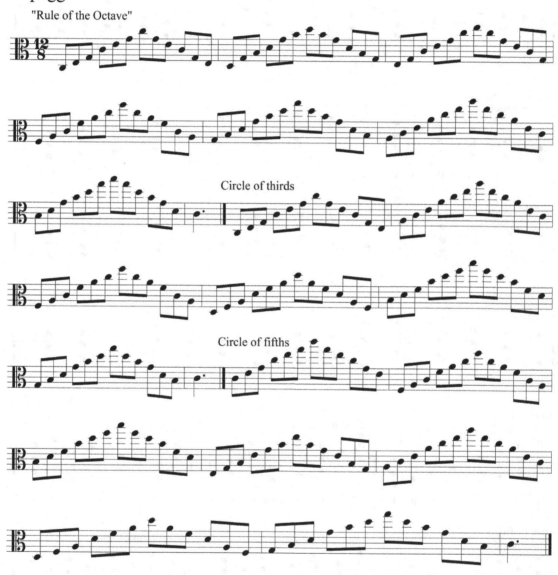

Circle of thirds

Circle of fifths

C minor

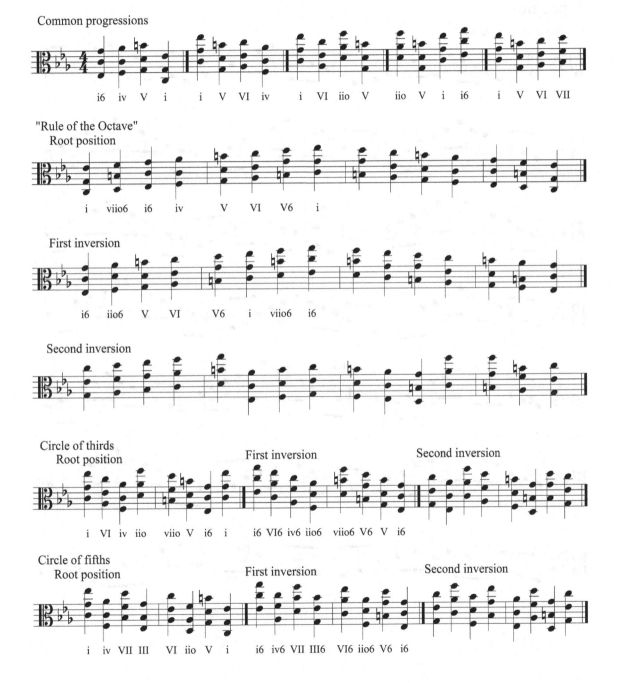

Arpeggios

"Rule of the Octave"

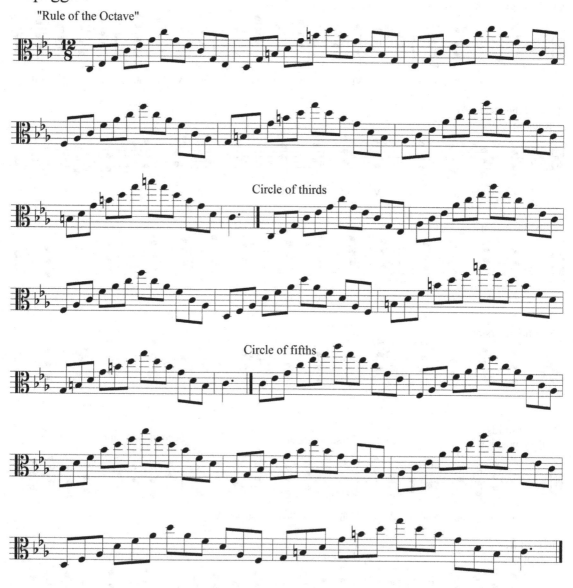

Circle of thirds

Circle of fifths

D♭ Major

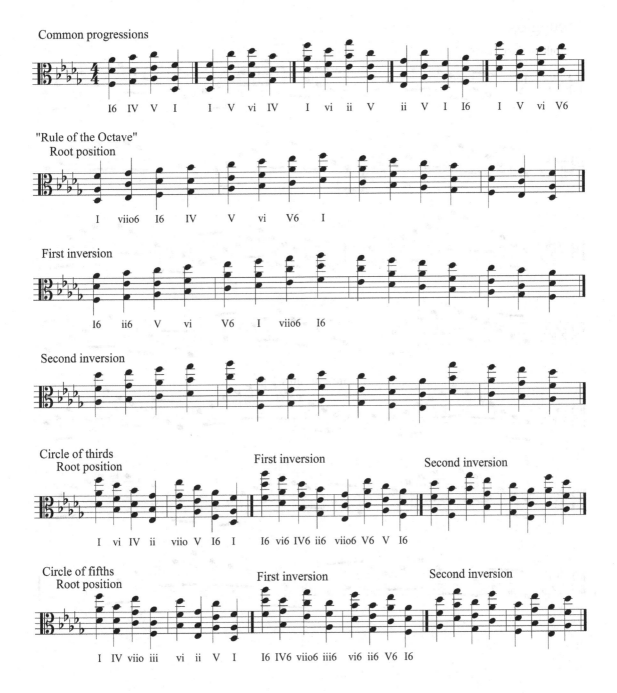

Arpeggios

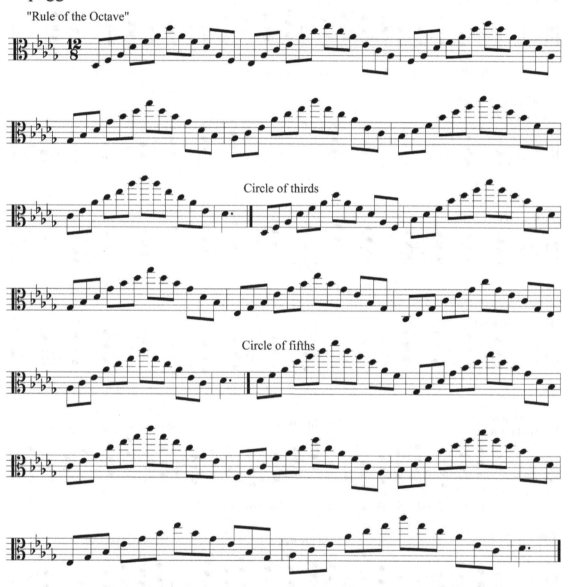

"Rule of the Octave"

Circle of thirds

Circle of fifths

C# Major

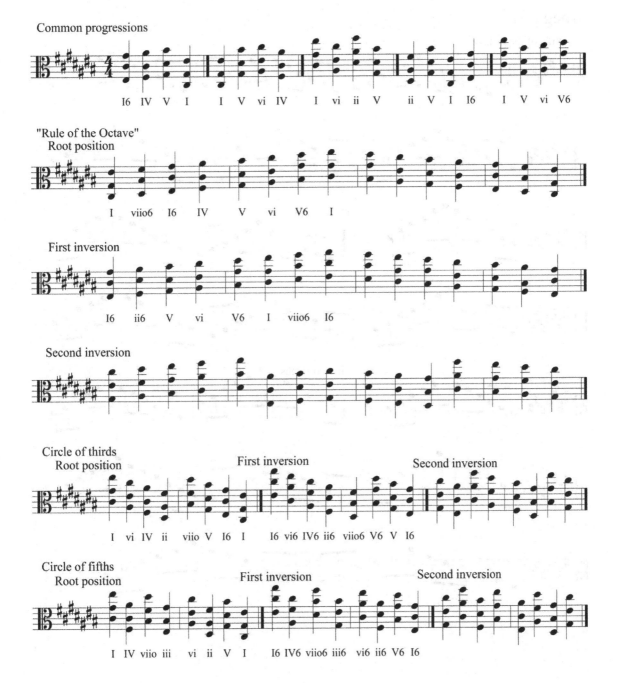

Arpeggios

"Rule of the Octave"

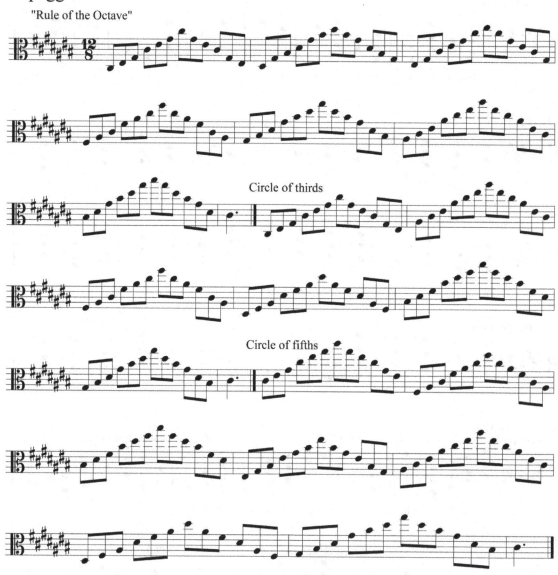

Circle of thirds

Circle of fifths

C# minor

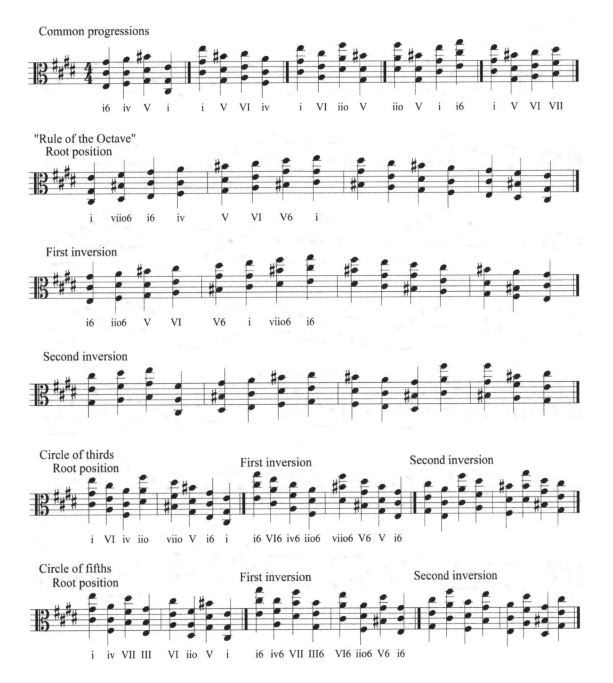

Arpeggios

"Rule of the Octave"

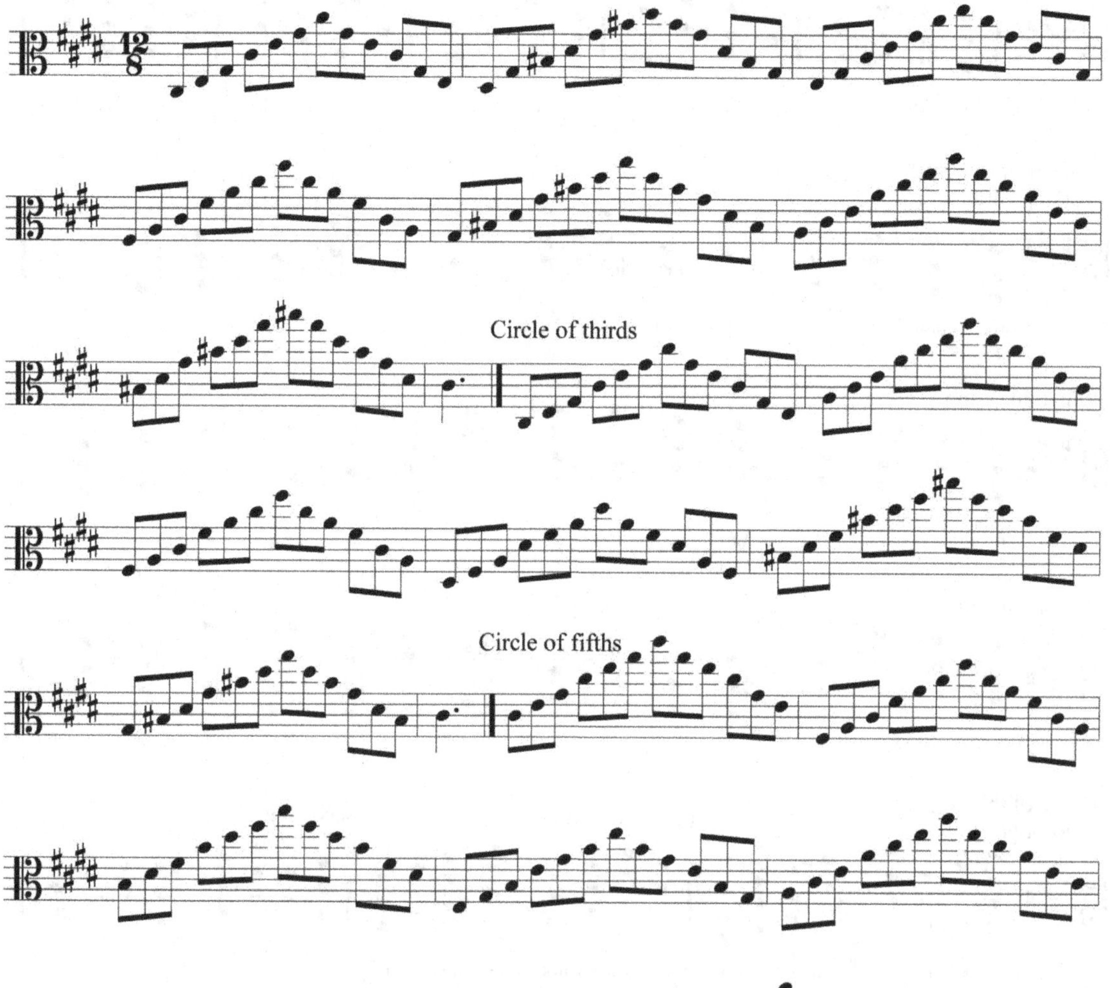

Circle of thirds

Circle of fifths

D Major

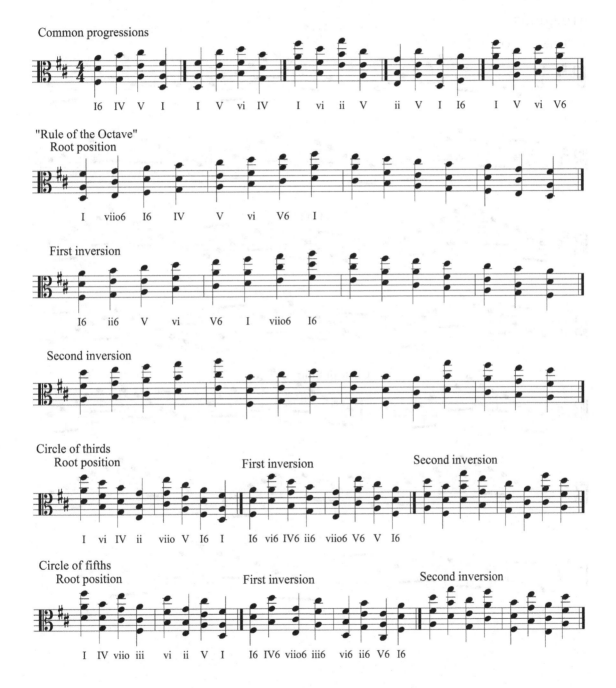

Arpeggios

"Rule of the Octave"

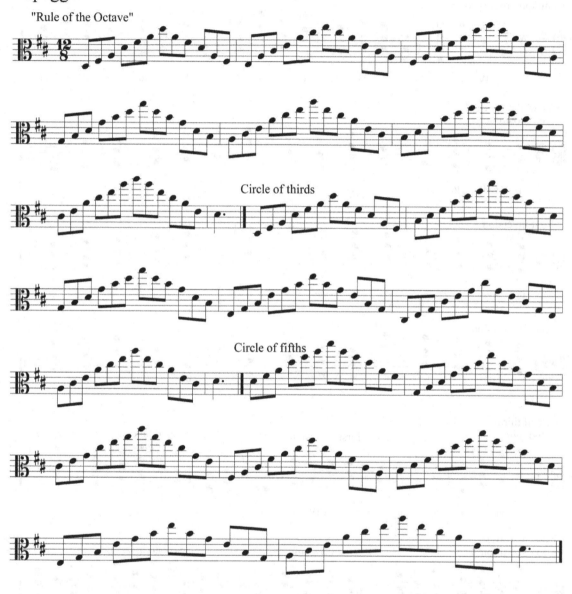

Circle of thirds

Circle of fifths

D minor

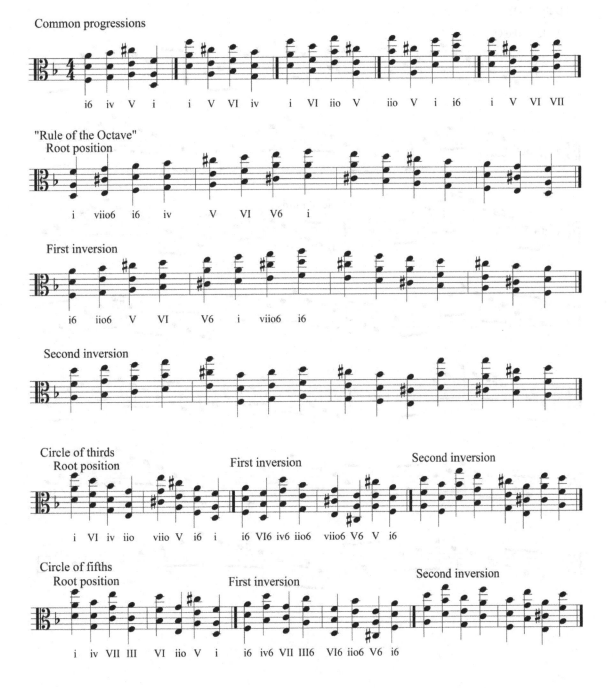

Arpeggios

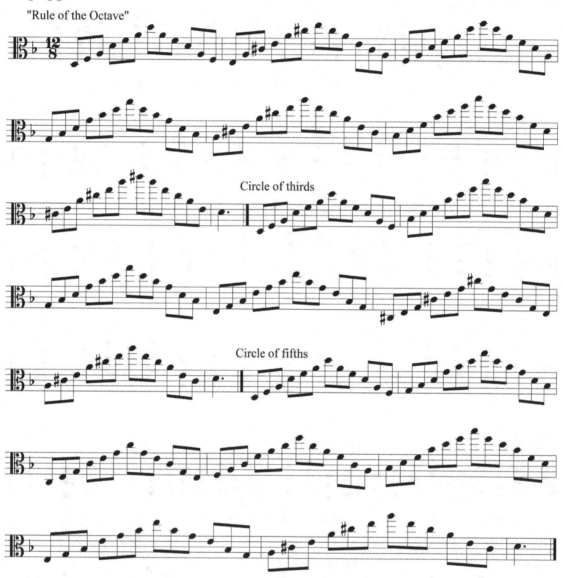

E♭ Major

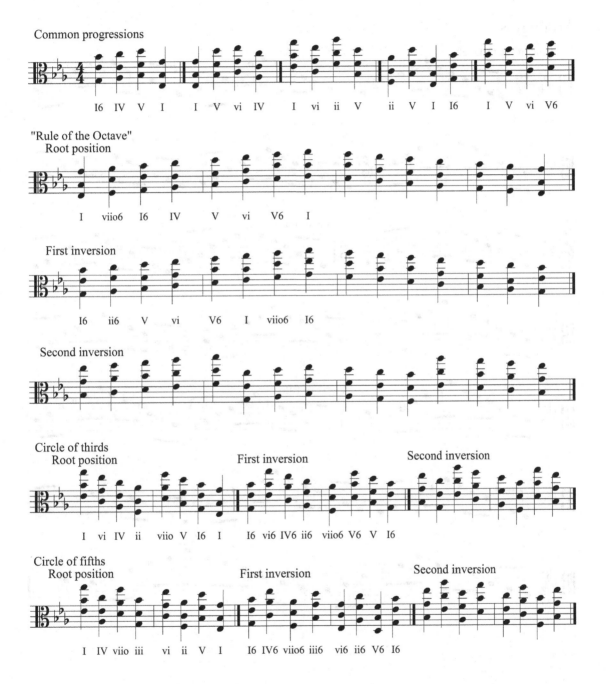

Arpeggios

"Rule of the Octave"

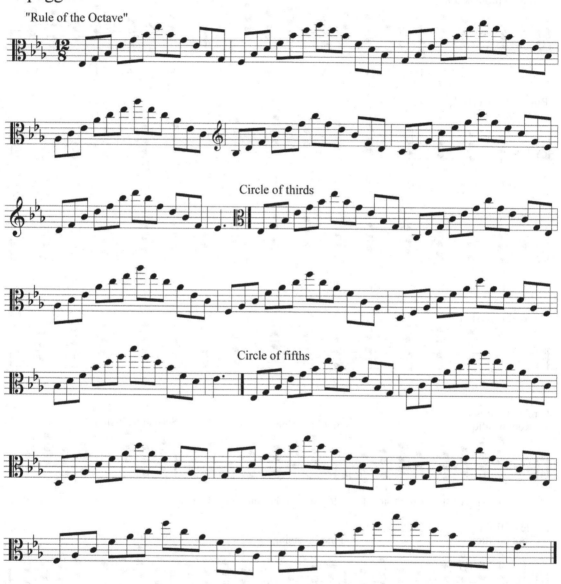

E♭ minor

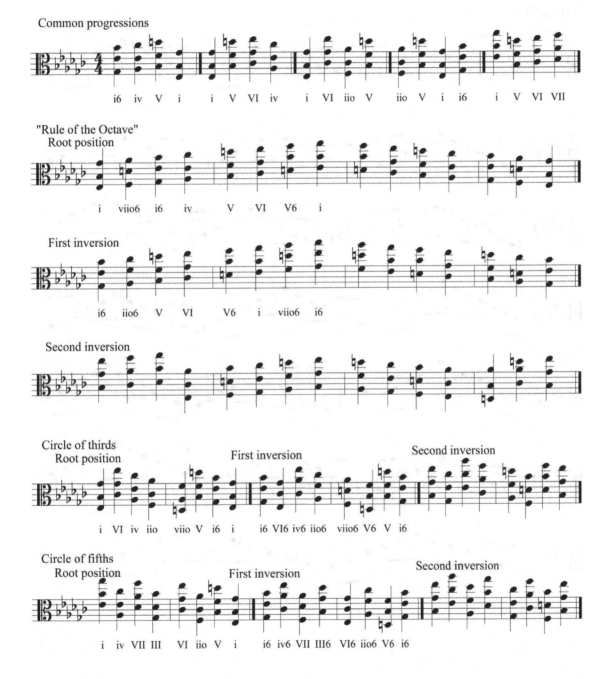

Arpeggios

"Rule of the Octave"

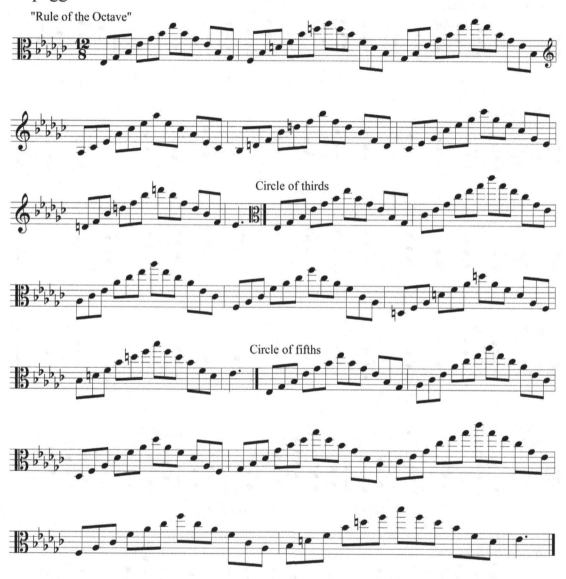

D# minor

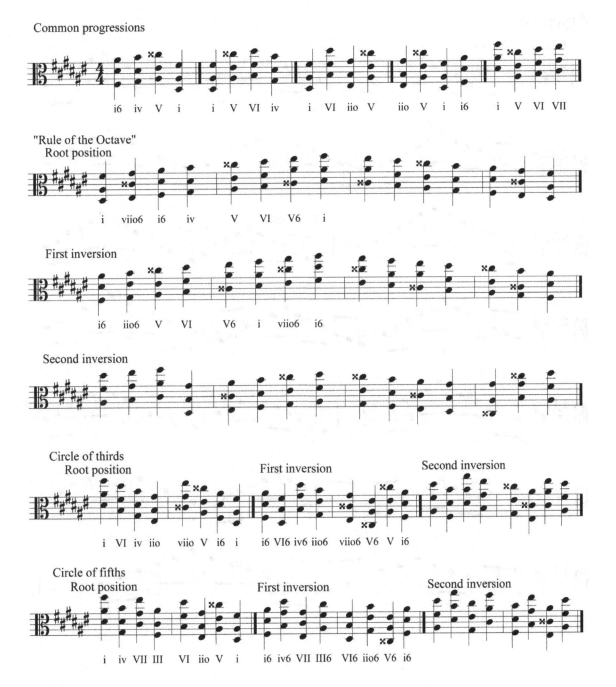

Arpeggios

"Rule of the Octave"

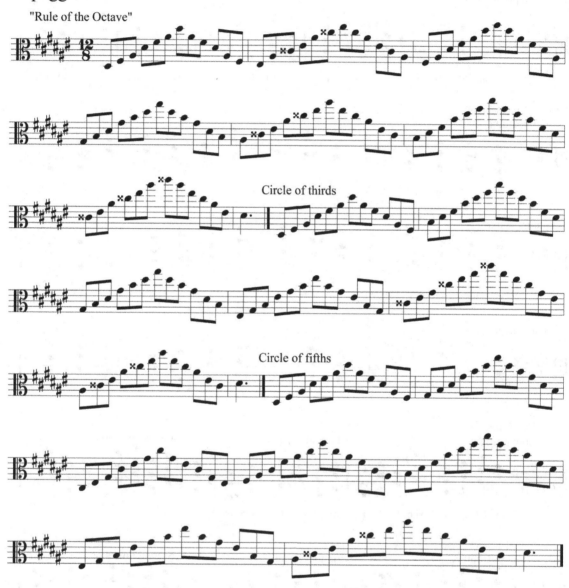

E Major

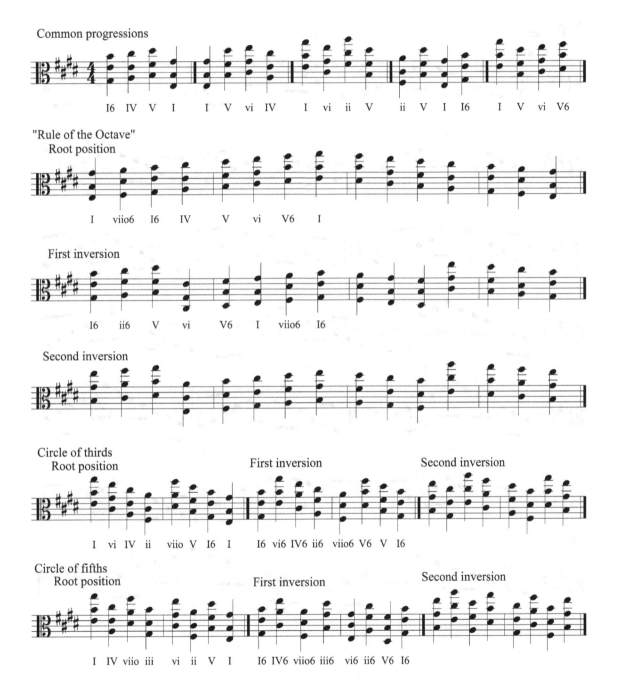

Arpeggios

"Rule of the Octave"

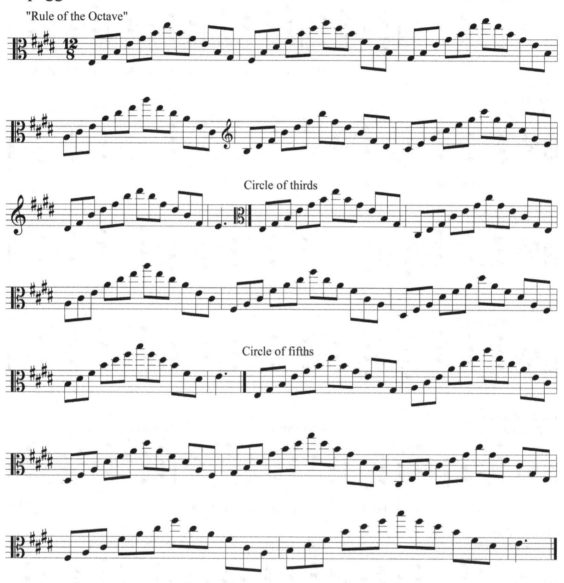

Circle of thirds

Circle of fifths

E minor

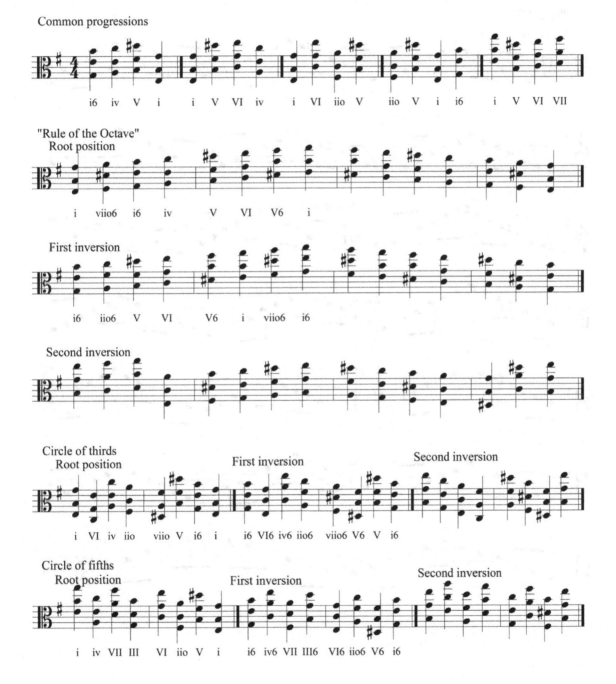

Arpeggios

"Rule of the Octave"

Circle of thirds

Circle of fifths

F Major

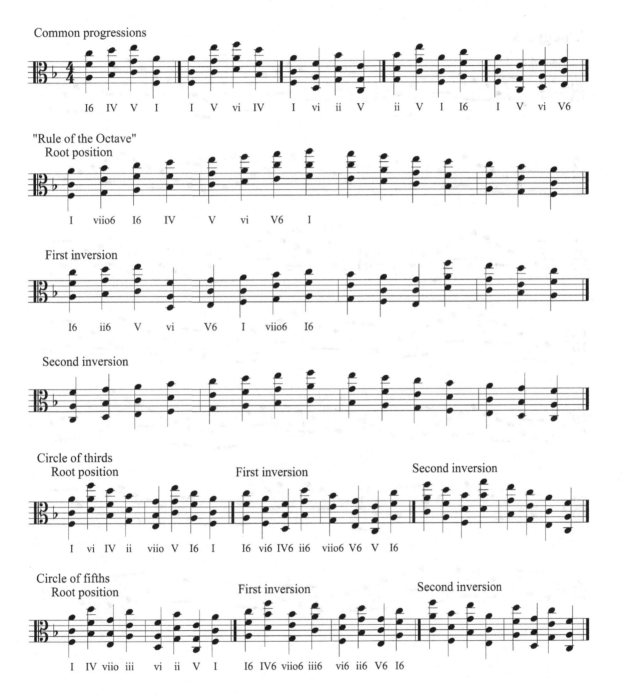

Arpeggios

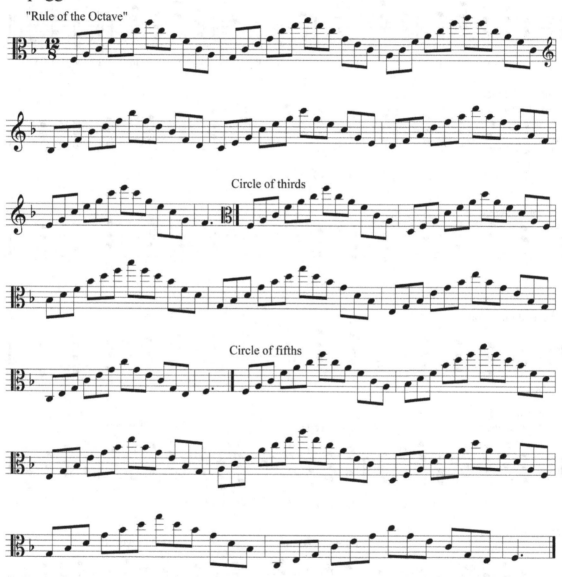

F minor

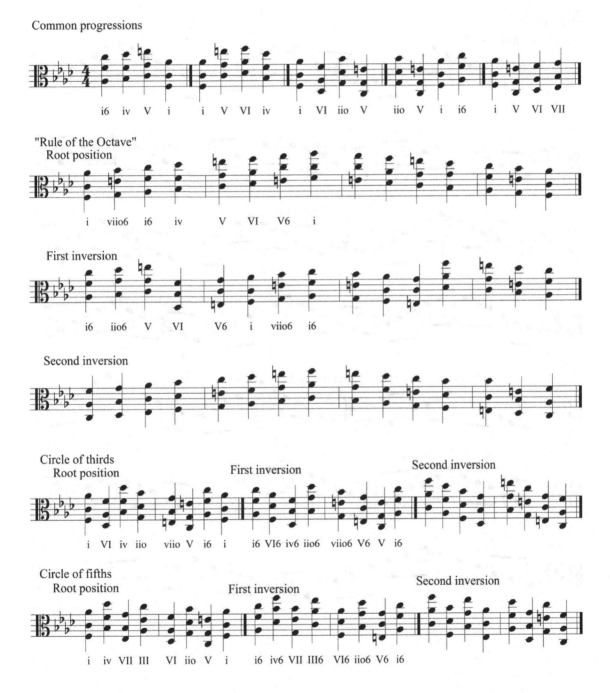

Arpeggios

"Rule of the Octave"

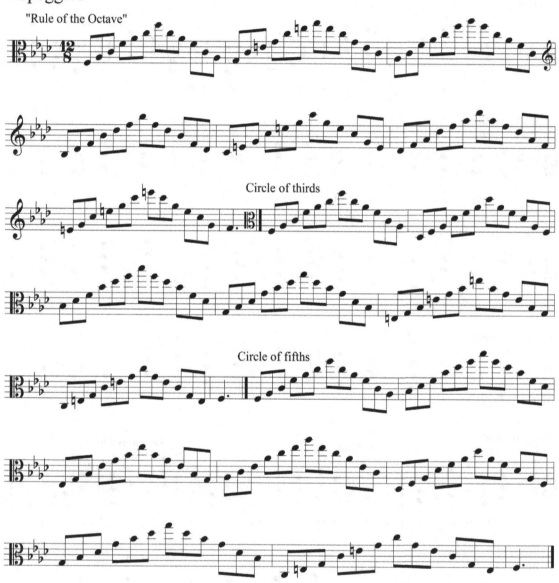

Circle of thirds

Circle of fifths

G♭ Major

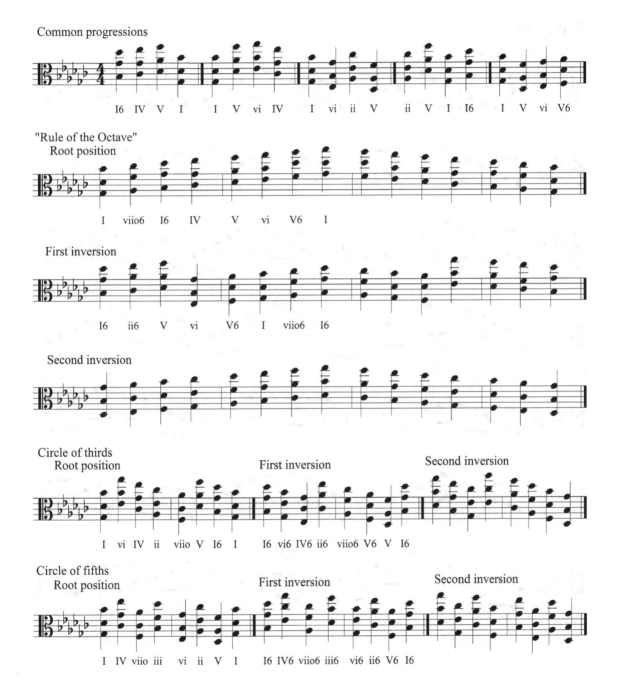

Arpeggios

"Rule of the Octave"

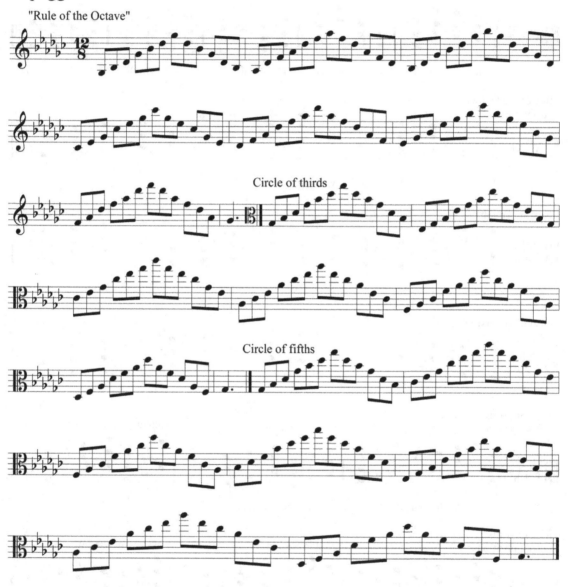

F# Major

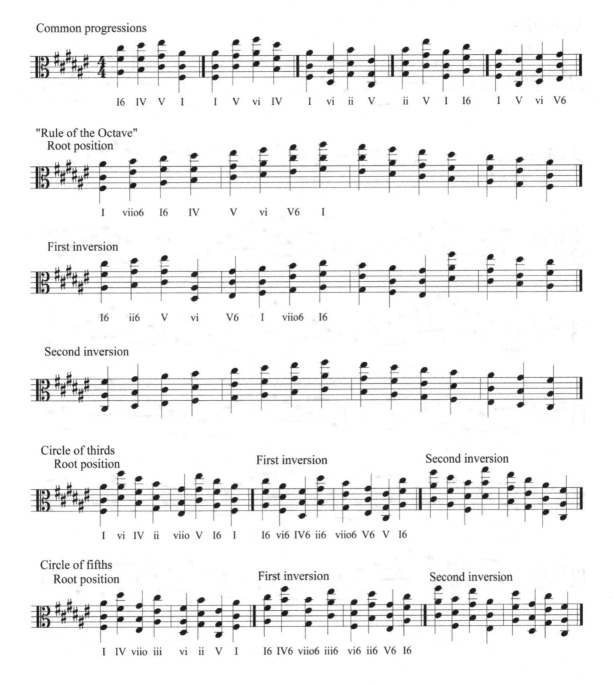

Arpeggios

"Rule of the Octave"

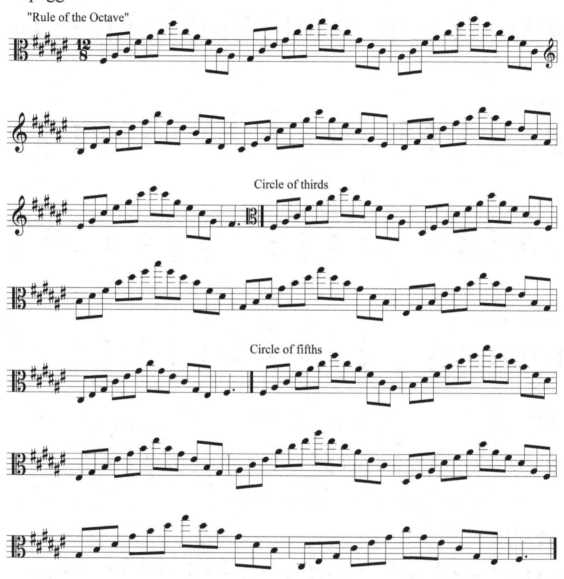

Circle of thirds

Circle of fifths

F# minor

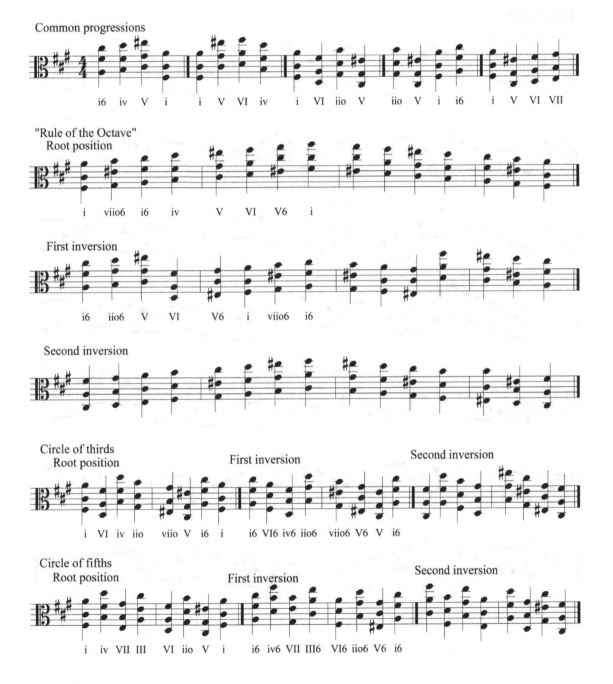

Arpeggios

"Rule of the Octave"

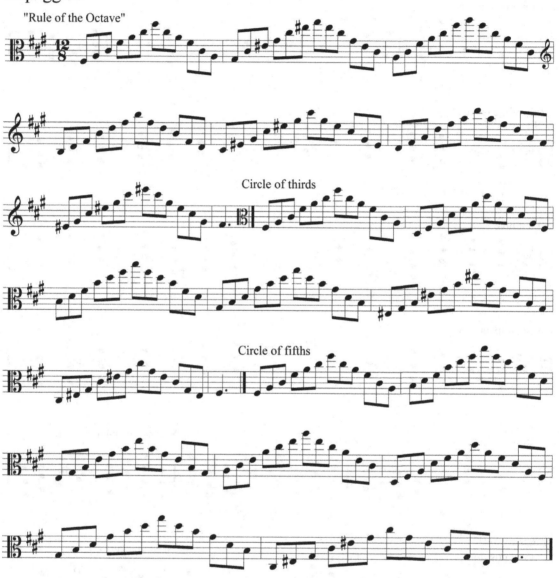

Circle of thirds

Circle of fifths

G Major

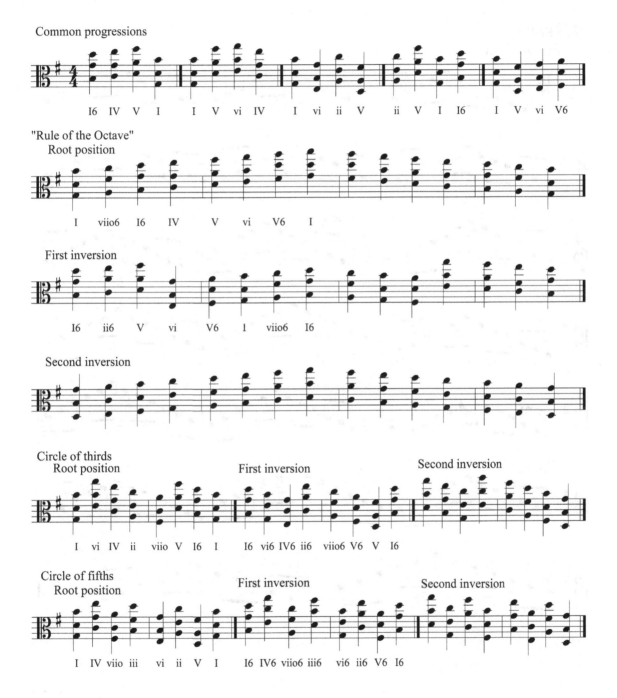

Arpeggios

"Rule of the Octave"

Circle of thirds

Circle of fifths

G minor

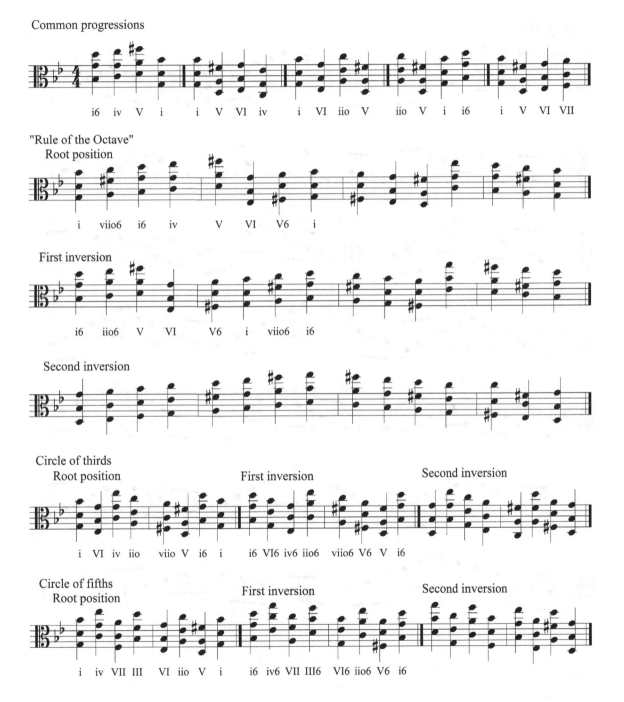

Arpeggios

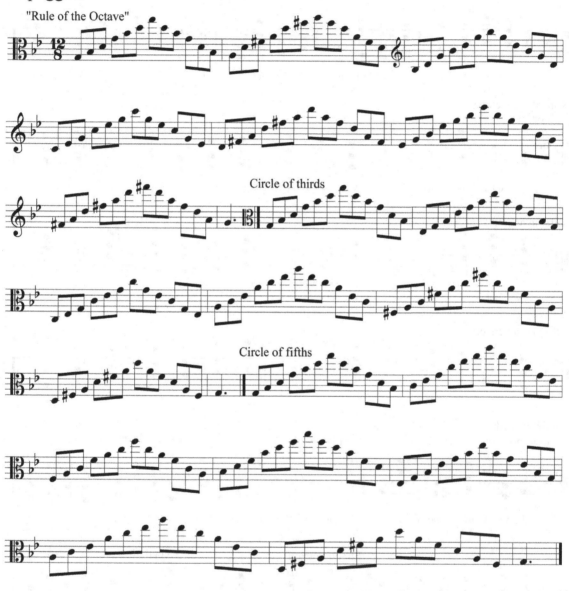

A♭ Major

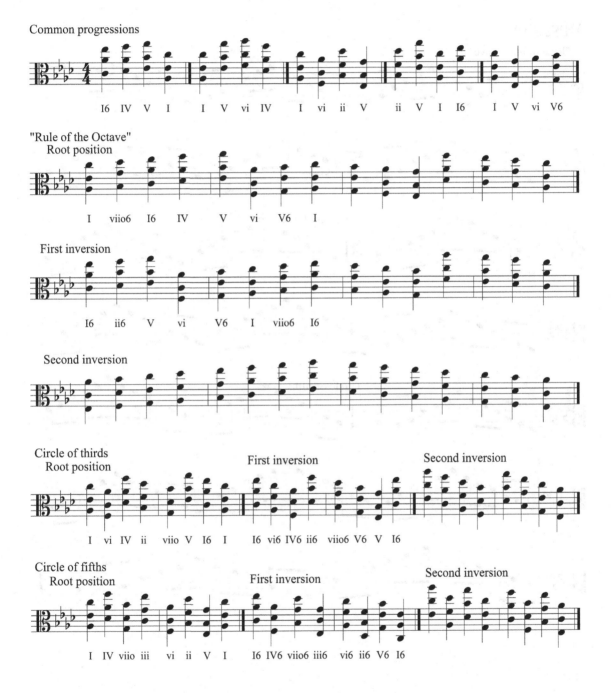

Arpeggios

"Rule of the Octave"

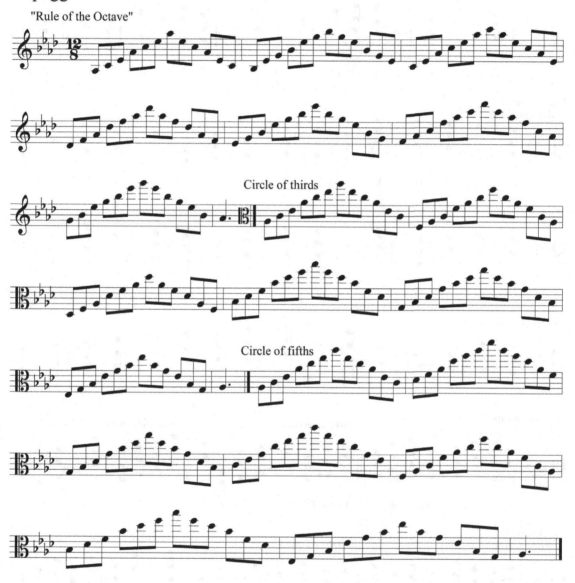

Circle of thirds

Circle of fifths

A♭ minor

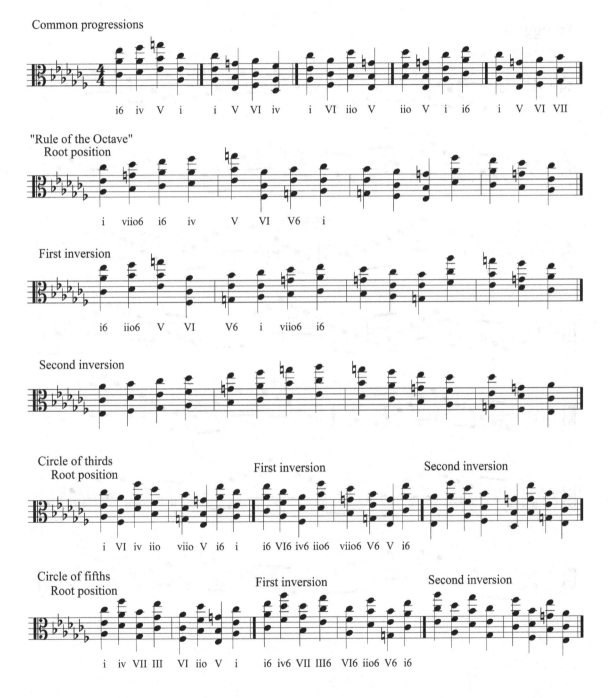

Arpeggios

"Rule of the Octave"

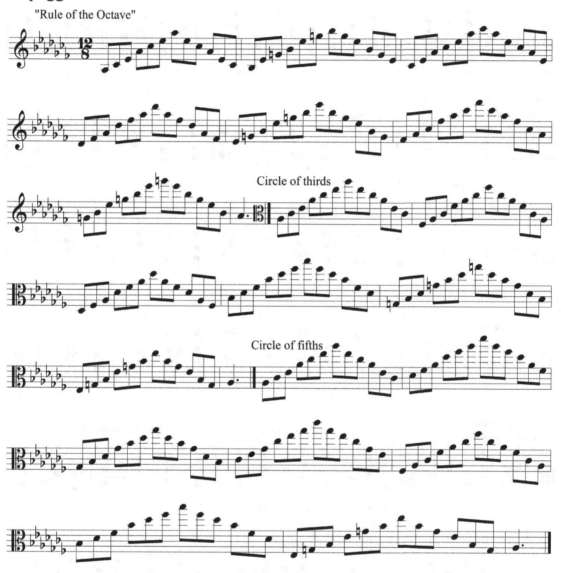

G# minor

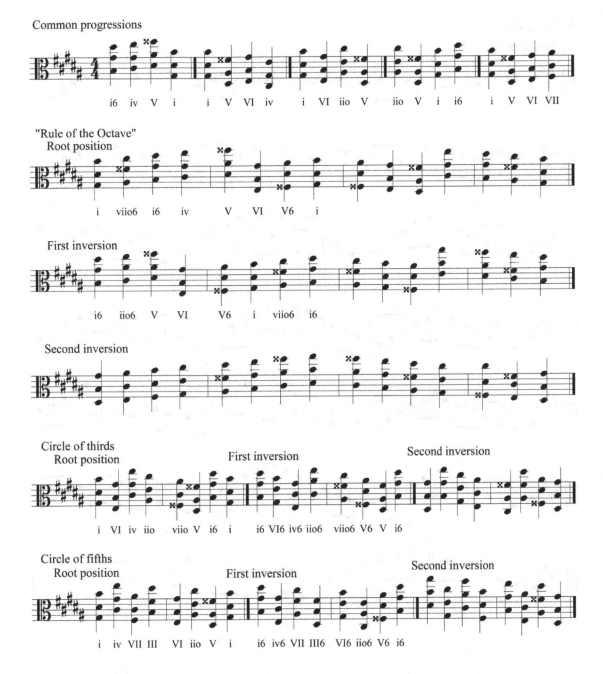

Arpeggios

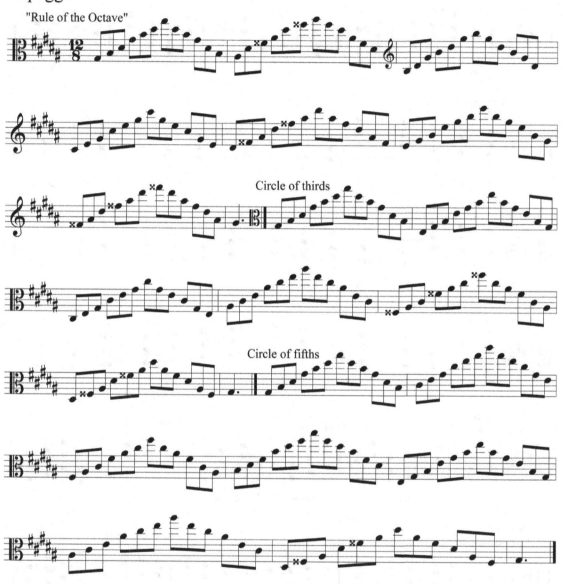

A Major

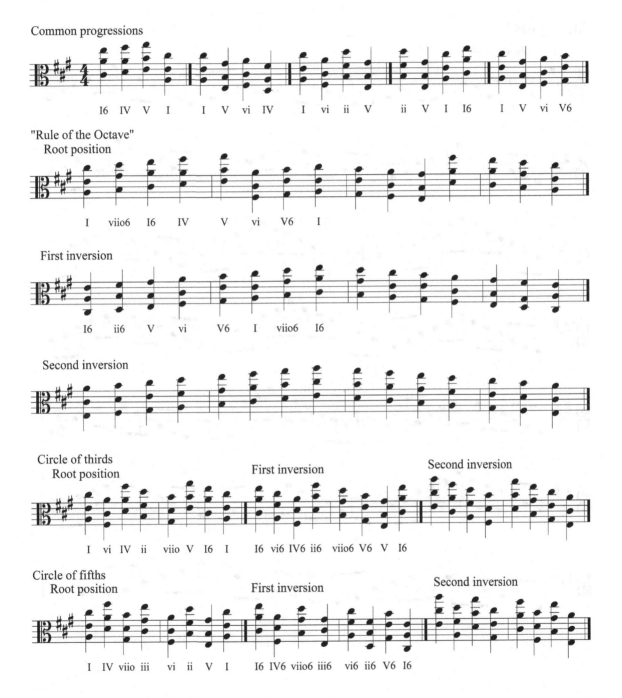

Arpeggios

"Rule of the Octave"

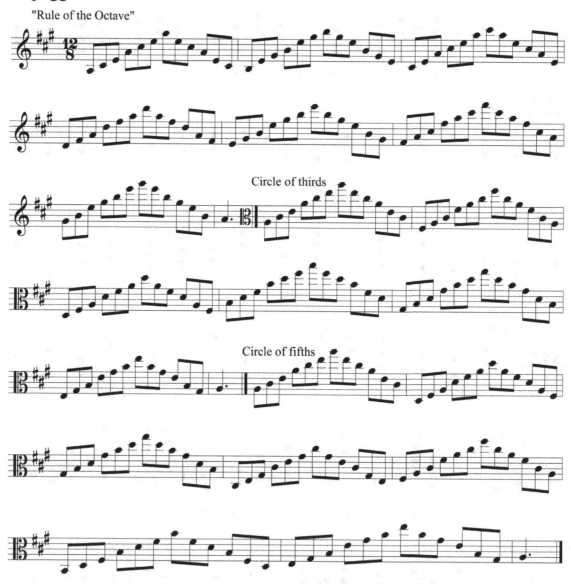

A minor

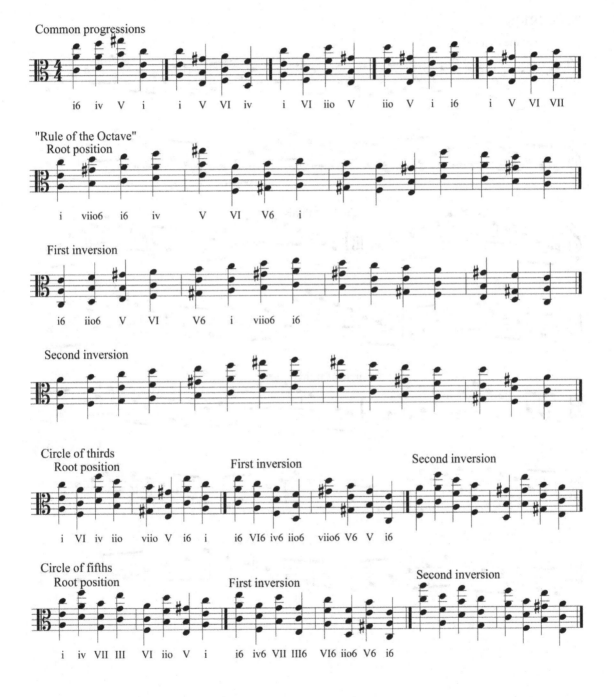

Arpeggios

"Rule of the Octave"

B♭ Major

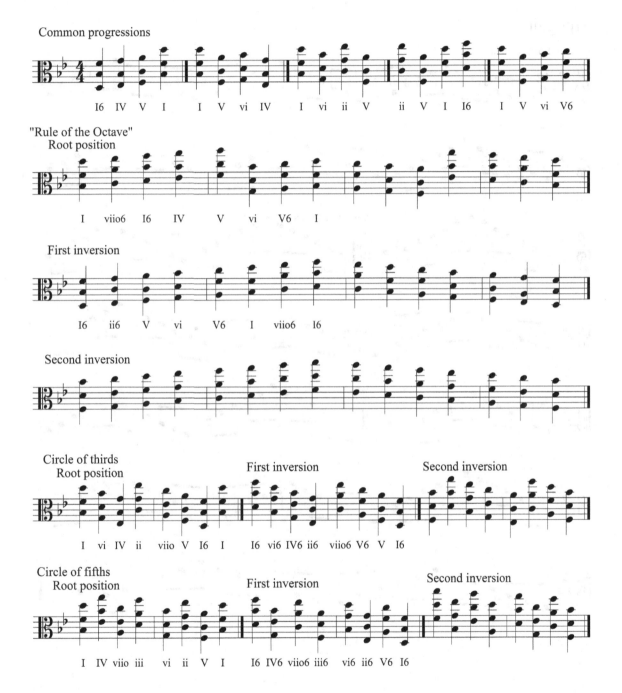

Arpeggios

"Rule of the Octave"

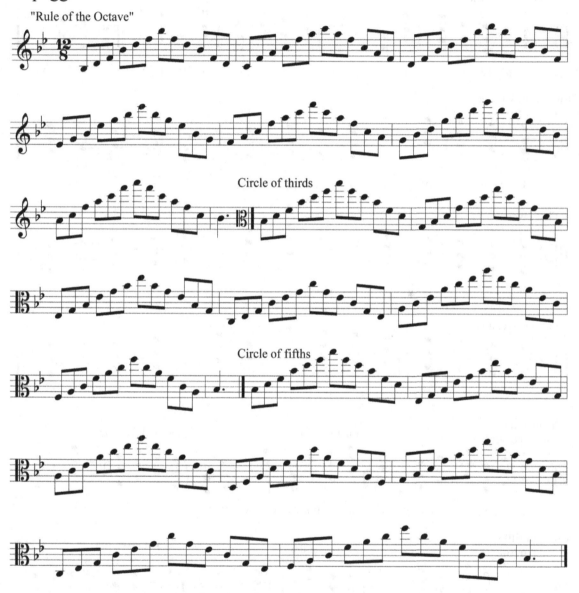

B♭ minor

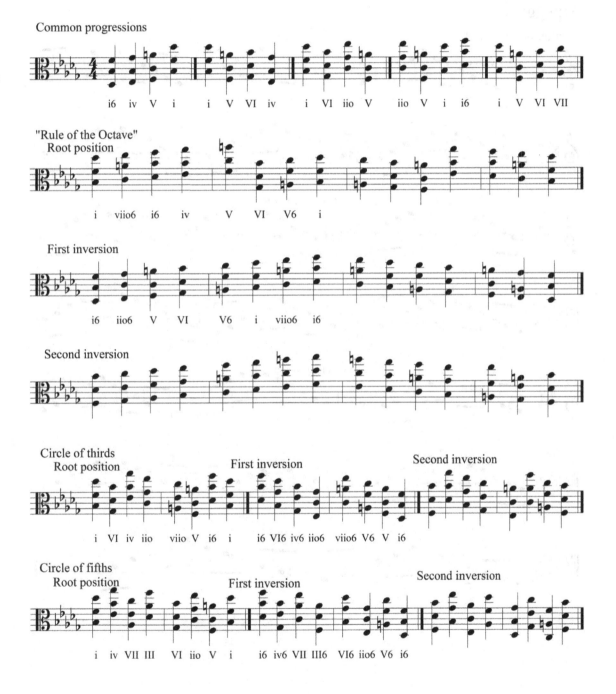

Arpeggios

"Rule of the Octave"

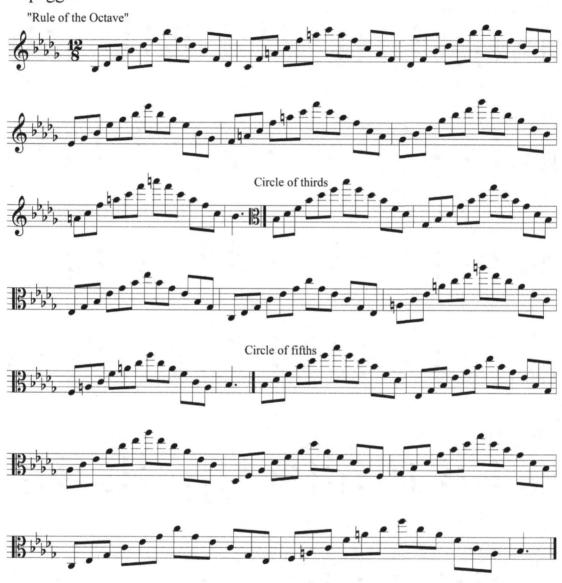

A# minor

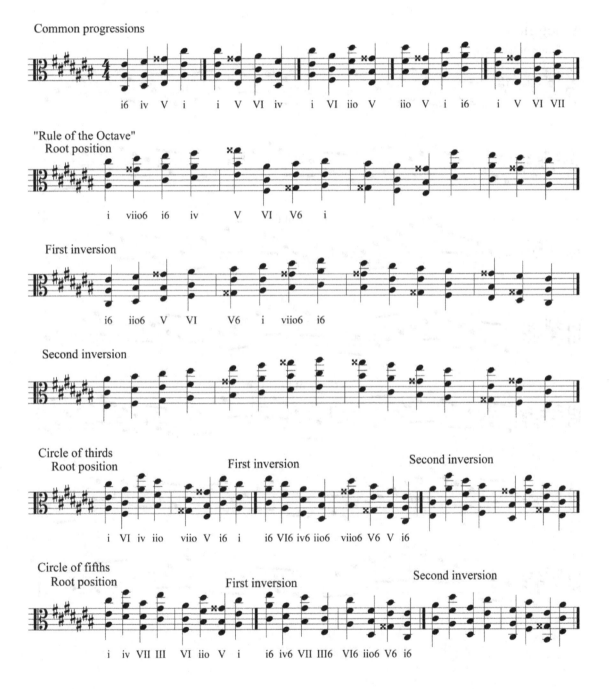

Arpeggios

"Rule of the Octave"

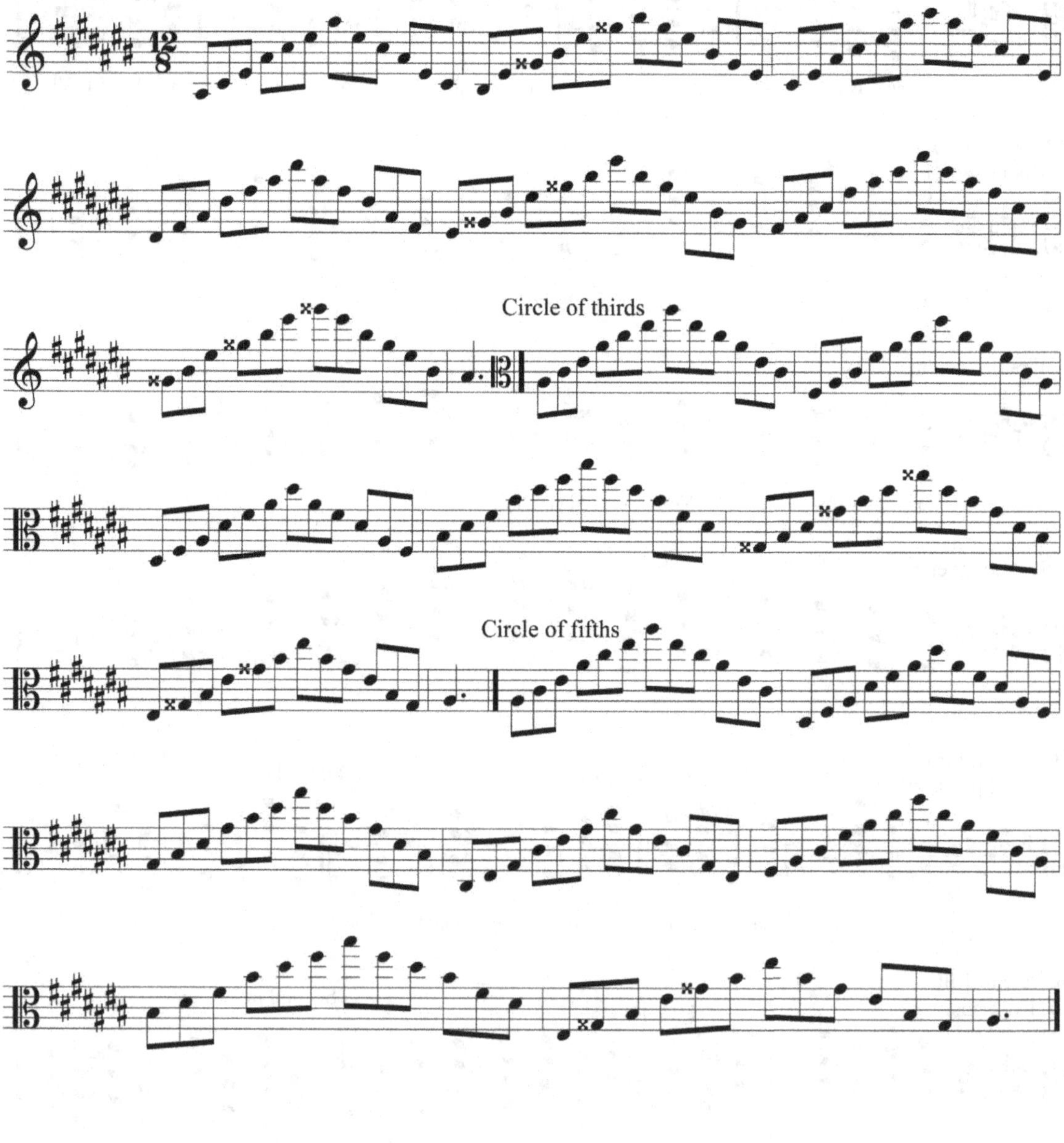

Circle of thirds

Circle of fifths

C♭ Major

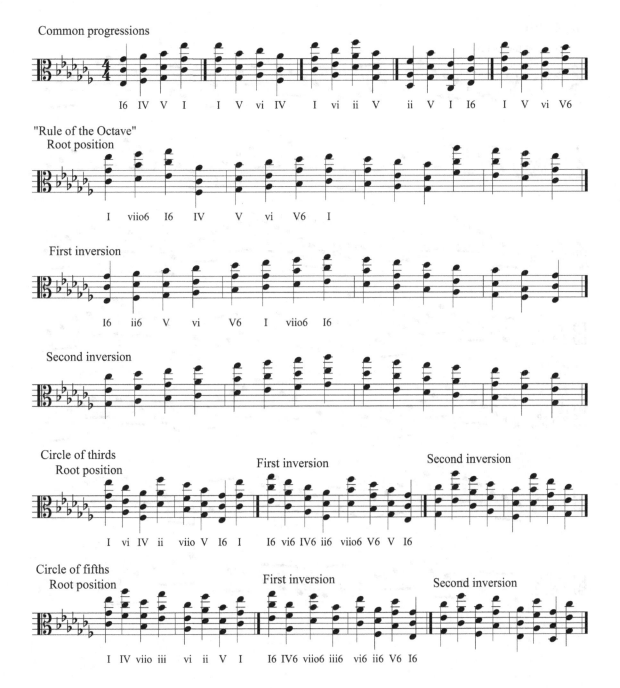

Arpeggios

"Rule of the Octave"

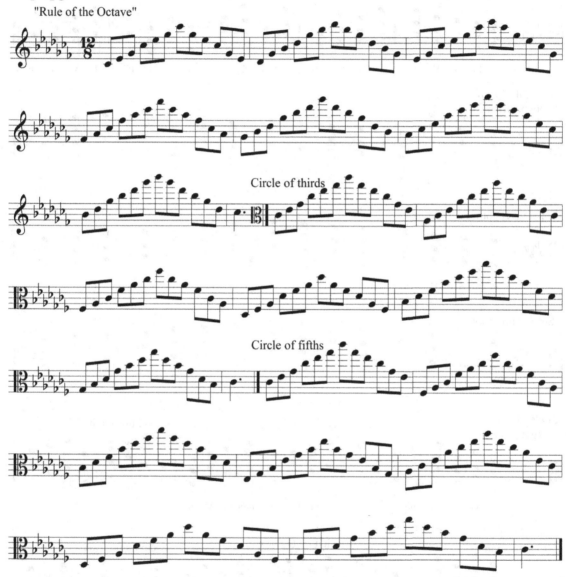

B Major

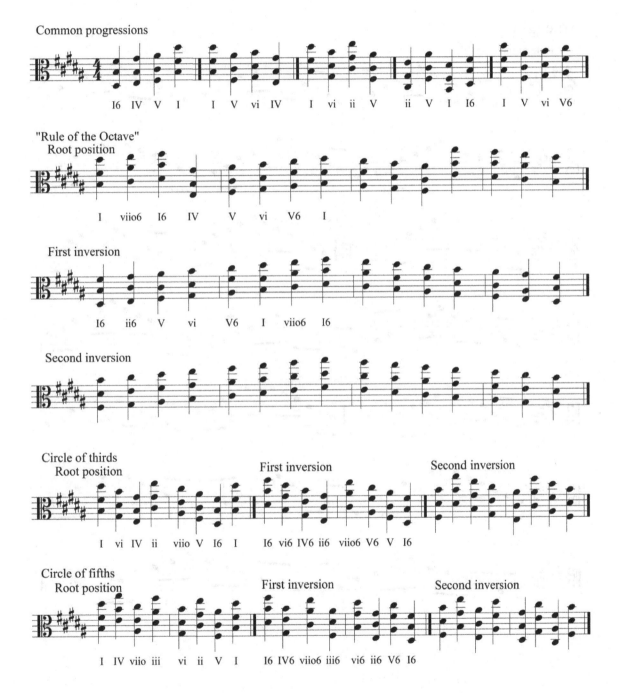

Arpeggios

"Rule of the Octave"

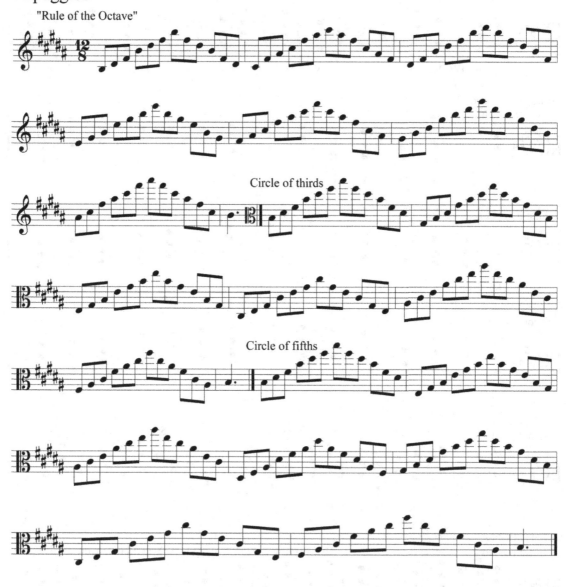

B minor

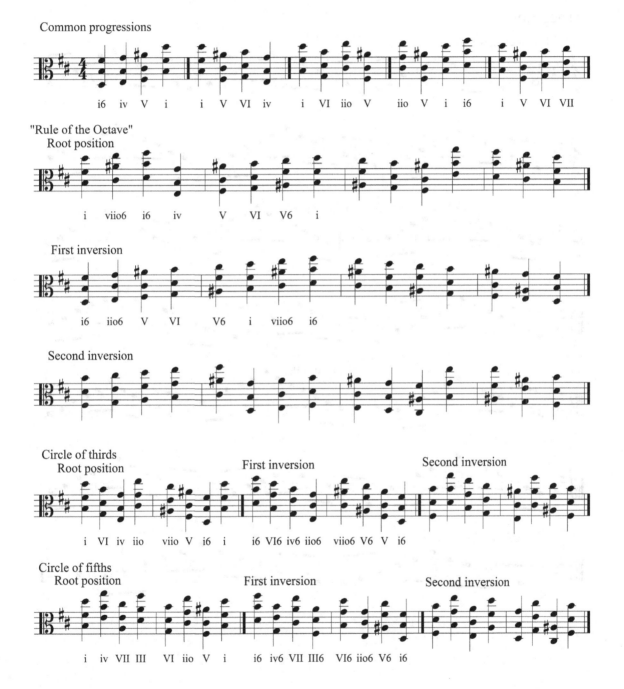

Arpeggios

"Rule of the Octave"

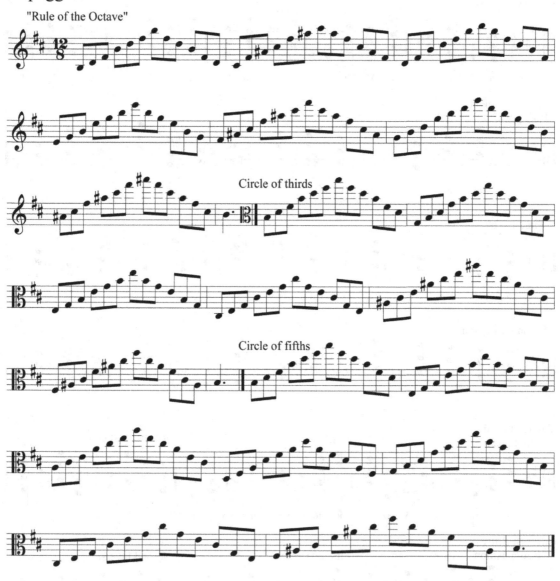

Part 3:

Further Applications

Double stops as chord progressions

Discussions of "chords" in Western music usually refers to triads, along with the occasional seventh chord. However, there are situations in which chords are implied through the use of just two pitches at a time (rather than three or more). This reduction to two voices is especially popular on an instrument like the viola, with its proclivity for playing one pitch at a time rather than being thought of as a truly "chordal" instrument.

If a member of the triad is to be omitted, it is usually the fifth. In other words, the two pitches present will be the root and the third of the chord. So, for example, a scale in double stop thirds can imply a series of root position chords, as follows:

while the same scale in sixths can be seen as implying a series of first-inversion chords:

There are other situations in the viola repertoire when we are playing on just two strings but still filling in all three notes of the chord, because on one of the strings we are alternating between two chord members. Below is an example of this idea with root position chords:

Try the same idea in a minor key:

The disadvantage of playing root-position chords in this manner is (1) the awkwardness of playing so many perfect fifths, and (2) the undesirable sound of these "parallel fifths" in terms of voice leading. As such, we are more likely to encounter the idea above with first inversion chords, such as is shown below in a major key:

and in a minor key:

While we are at it, let's take a look at what this sort of approach would look like with augmented triads:

Diminished triads tend to be a little bit more flexible in their voicing, so below I have shown three different ways that you might encounter these chords on two strings:

Finally, below are two voicings in which you might encounter dominant seventh chords on two strings:

High registers

If you are using this book, there's a good chance that you are already used to playing in high registers on the viola. However, it wouldn't hurt to see what some of the preceding materials look like in higher registers.

First, here is a scale in thirds in treble clef:

Here is a similar scale in sixths:

Sometimes we encounter the idea of triads on two strings in high registers as well. For example, below are root-position triads on two strings in treble clef in a major key:

And in a minor key:

Sometimes we find a similar figuration, but with the fifth omitted and the root doubled, such as the following:

Here are two versions of first-inversion triads in treble clef, in a major key:

And in a minor key:

The fingering pattern for any of the above figurations should be easily transposed into any other key, and I hope that you will consider doing so.

Sometimes we may encounter, or otherwise want to play, chords on three strings in higher registers. Here is what the "rule of the octave" progression looks like in root position in C major:

And in C minor:

Here is the rule of the octave in first inversion, first in major:

And in minor:

Rule of the octave, second inversion, in major:

And in minor:

Here are all the diminished triads and seventh chords, in three different voicings:

Here is an octave's worth of augmented triads:

Here is the same idea but with dominant seventh chords. Again, three different voicings are shown:

Modulation

Understanding chords means learning to think *harmonically*. Another facet of harmony is the topic of *modulation*—the process of changing keys or tonal centers.

In much of Western music, the most common type of modulation is one that takes us to a "closely related key." The closely related keys are the keys of the other chords that are diatonic to the starting key, which in major keys are those of the ii, iii, IV, V, and vi chords, and in minor keys are to the III, iv, v, VI, and VII chords.

Let us look at a few examples of modulations in their simplest forms, starting with one to the key of the dominant (i.e., the V chord):

In the end, to get from G major to D major we need to add C#'s (^#4 in the original key). However, to further reduce the tendency to hear G as tonic, try introducing G#'s as well (^#1 in the original key).

Here is an example of a modulation to the subdominant (the IV chord):

To accomplish this modulation, add ^b7.

Modulations to the submediant will need to involve ^#5. For example:

To modulate to the mediant, we need ^#2:

To modulate to the supertonic, add ^#1:

In the past century, it is not uncommon to find a modulation to a key that is a half step higher than the present tonic. Below is one example of how you might accomplish such a key change:

Still another type of modulation is the *common tone* modulation, which uses a pitch that is common between two key as a "pivot pitch," if you will. This sort of modulation is sometimes used to change the key by a third, but to a key that is not closely related to the starting key (i.e., "chromatic mediant" modulations). Below is one such example:

In order to become more familiar with these modulations, try transposing them to all other keys.

Allow me to reiterate that the above discussion is but the briefest of introductions to the topic of modulation. If you have aspirations of composing, improvising, or even analyzing music, you will want to become skilled and well-versed at the subject, which means:

- Devising many examples of modulations of your own.
- Exploring additional reading materials on the subject, some of which can be found in the bibliography.
- Listening to and studying as much modulating music as you can.
- Perhaps taking some composition lessons.

Quiz

After spending this much time with chords on the viola, let's see how quickly you can create these chords. Below is a quiz consisting of groups of four chords in various keys. The number 6 by a chord means "first inversion," and the numbers 6/4 by a chord means "second inversion." Compare the chords you devise with the answer key on the following pages. Try taking the quiz with a metronome set at a moderate or slow tempo, and consider recording yourself so that you can later confirm which chords you played.

Major keys

1. E major — iii vi ii V
2. F major — vi IV ii viio
3. D major — I iii vi V
4. G major — I vi IV V
5. Bb major — I V^6_4 I6 V
6. A major — iii vi ii V
7. C# major — I iii IV V
8. Eb major — I vi IV V
9. Cb major — I iii IV V
10. Gb major — I ii vi V
11. Db major — I V vi IV
12. F# major — I ii vi V
13. B major — I iii vi V
14. C major — I V vi IV
15. Ab major — I V^6_4 I6 V

Minor keys

1. C# minor — i III iv V
2. A minor — i V^6_4 i6 V
3. D# minor — i III VI V
4. Eb minor — VI iv iio viio
5. C minor — i V VI iv
6. B minor — i VI iv V
7. G minor — i V^6_4 i6 V
8. Ab minor — i III VI V
9. D minor — III VI iio V
10. F# minor — i VI iv V
11. G# minor — i iio VI V
12. E minor — i V VI iv
13. F minor — III VI iio V
14. Bb minor — i III iv V
15. A# minor — i iio VI V

Solutions

Major keys

1. E major   iii vi ii V

2. F# major   vi IV ii viio

3. D major   I iii vi V

4. G major   I vi IV V

5. Bb major   I V$^6_4$ I6 V

6. A major   iii vi ii V

7. C# major   I iii IV V

8. Eb major   I vi IV V

9. Cb major   I iii IV V

10. Gb major   I ii vi V

11. Db major   I V vi IV

12. F major   I ii vi V

13. B major   I iii vi V

14. C major   I V vi IV

15. Ab major   I V$^6_4$ I6 V

Minor keys

1. C# minor   i III iv V

2. A minor   i V$^6_4$ i6 V

3. D# minor   i III VI V

4. Eb minor   VI iv iio viio

5. G minor   i V VI iv

6. Bb minor   i VI iv V

7. C minor   i V$^6_4$ i6 V

8. Ab minor   i III VI V

9. D minor   III VI iio V

10. F# minor   i VI iv V

11. G# minor   i iio VI V

12.   E minor   i V VI iv

13.   F minor   III VI iio V

14.   B minor   i III iv V

15.   A# minor   i iio VI V

Bibliography

Theory Textbooks

Aldwell, Edward, and Carl Schachter. *Harmony and Voice Leading*. Boston, MA. Schirmer. 2010.

Burstein, L. Poundie and Joseph N. Straus. *Concise Introduction to Tonal Harmony*. New York: W.W. Norton, 2016.

Kostka, Stefan and Dorothy Payne. *Tonal Harmony*, 6th ed. New York: McGraw-Hill, 2008.

Ottman, Robert W. *Advanced Harmony: Theory and Practice*, 5th ed. Upper Saddle River, NJ: Prentice Hall, 2000.

Piston, Walter and Mark DeVoto. *Harmony*, 5th ed. New York: W.W. Norton, 1987.

Schroeder, Carl and Keith Wyatt. *Harmony and Theory: A Comprehensive Source for All Musicians*. Los Angeles: Musicians Institute Press, 1998.

Jazz Theory

Hellmer, Jeffrey and Lawn, Richard. *Jazz Theory and Practice: For Performers, Composers, and Arrangers*. University of Texas – Austin. Alfred Music. 2005.

LeVine, Mark. *The Jazz Theory Book*. Petaluma, CA. Sher Music. 1995

Ligon, Bert. *Jazz Theory Resources: Volume 1*. Texas. Houston Publishing, Inc. 2001.

Rule of the octave

Rameau, Jean-Phillipe. *Generation Harmonique*. Paris. Prault fils. 1737.

Rameau, Jean-Phillipe. *Treatise on Harmony*. Paris. J.B.C. Ballard. 1722.

Surmani, Andrew and Karen Farnum and Manus, Morton. *Alfred's Essentials of Music Theory: Complete Book Alto Clef (Viola) Edition*. Texas. Alfred Music. 1999.

Miscellaneous

Reger, Max. *Modulation*. Dover Publications. 2007.

Whitcomb, Benjamin. *"Creating Your Own Cadenzas,"* The Instrumentalist. Fall 2013.

Biography

Benjamin Whitcomb lives with his wife, Pamela, and twin sons in Fort Atkinson, Wisconsin. Benjamin was born in Florida, but spent most of his childhood in Stillwater, Oklahoma. He attended Oklahoma State University (BM, cello performance), Boston University, and the University of Texas at Austin (MM, cello performance; PhD, music theory), and he has studied with Evan Tonsing, George Neikrug, and Phyllis Young.

Benjamin and Pamela moved to Wisconsin in 1999 when Benjamin joined the faculty of the University of Wisconsin-Whitewater, where he is currently Professor of Cello and Music Theory. Benjamin performs frequently in solo and chamber music recitals. He is a member of the Madison-based Ancora String Quartet (www.ancoraquartet.com) and the UW-W Piano Trio. He has also been a member several orchestras in Texas and Wisconsin. Benjamin frequently performs duo recitals around the country and abroad with pianist Vincent de Vries.

Benjamin's primary area of research is string pedagogy. Numerous articles of his have been published in such journals as *American String Teacher*, *Strings*, *Stringendo* (the journal of AUSTA), *The Instrumentalist*, and *Theoria*. He is a contributing author to *Sharpen Your String Technique* and to *Teaching Music through Performance in Orchestra*, vol. 3, and chaired the committee that revised the cello portion of the most recent *ASTA String Syllabus*. He has presented papers, masterclasses, and workshops at universities and conferences throughout the United States and abroad. His other books, *Cello Fingerings*, *Bass Fingerings*, and *The Advancing String Player's Handbooks* series, have received rave reviews and are available for through your favorite online bookstore.

Benjamin can be reached by email at whitcomb@uww.edu or through his website, www.benjaminwhitcomb.com.

Printed in the United States
By Bookmasters